Rustling Leaves

Aathiran

Rustling Leaves

Haiku Poems in English

சலசலக்கும் இலைகள்

Author: Aathiran©

Copyright: Author

First Edition: September 2024

Size: 5.5” x 8.5”

Inner Paper: Art Maplitho paper, 90 gsm

Pages: 124

ISBN No.: **978-93-340-9847-1**

Designed by: **Dr. R. Arulraj**

Published by

Maple Pathippagam, India

Dr. R. Arulraj (Aathiran)

97A, Fifth Cross Street, Thirumal Nagar,

Puducherry 605013, India

aathiran108@gmail.com; What’s App: +91 8870838964

Singapore

Dr. R. Arulraj (Aathiran)

Block 9, #07-30, Selegie Road, Singapore 180009.

Canada

Dr. R. Arulraj (Aathiran)

110, Lilian Drive, Scarborough, Ontario, Canada, M1R3W5

Printed at

Shri Vignesh Prints, Ashok Nagar, Chennai - 600 083.

Price: $ 10 / S$ 15 / CAD 15 / ₹ 200

To the lovely nature

OFFICE OF FORMER VICE-PRESIDENT

P. PILLAY VYAPOORY, GOSK

REPUBLIC OF MAURITIUS

66B. Sir Virgile Naz Avenue, Quatre Bornes

Tel: 454 2521, Mobile: 5256 8145

Congratulations to you, Aathiran (Dr. R. Arulraj), for that bright idea of composing Haiku poems in English.

This Japanese style of poetry, in praise of the dance of beauty in the natural world and by virtue of its conciseness and rhythm, does indeed appeal to our human heart and soul.

Beauty is in the eye of the beholder, and only poets can translate what is in the mind's eye into words, and the Haiku style lends itself beautifully to this process.

Aathiran, I really enjoyed reading your Haiku poems "Rustling Leaves".

Among others, your Haikus

"Rain cleared-
In leaves rustling
It's rain again"

"Spread with enumerous stars,
Lo, fireflies all over
The dark jungle"

"Till it reaches nostrils–
Fragrance of flowers,
Transmitted by wind – not known!"

have indeed, as you expect, guided me to a place of stillness and contemplation, where the noise of the world fades and the subtle music of life comes forward.

Well done, Aathiran.
I look forward to reading your future compositions.

13-08-2024

P. Pillay Vyapoory, GOSK.

Preface

Rustling Leaves...

The tradition of haiku has deep roots in Japanese culture, with masters like Matsuo Basho, Yosa Buson, and Kobayashi Issa offering timeless contributions that continue to resonate across centuries and cultures. Their works capture moments of profound simplicity and beauty, often with a touch of poignant insight.

Matsuo Basho, the most revered haiku poet, wrote:

An old silent pond...
A frog jumps into the pond-
Splash! Silence again.

In these few words, Basho encapsulates a serene moment in nature, a sudden disturbance, and the return to calm-a metaphor for the fleeting nature of life itself. His haiku invite readers to find tranquility and reflection in the midst of daily chaos.

Yosa Buson, another haiku master, offered vivid imagery with a painter's eye:

Light of the moon
Moves west, flowers' shadows
Creep eastward.

Buson's haiku highlights the delicate interplay of light and shadow, illustrating how even the moon's subtle movements can create a dance of beauty in the natural world. His poems remind us to appreciate the subtle changes that occur around us every day.
Kobayashi Issa, known for his compassionate and often whimsical verses, wrote:

The snow is melting
And the village is flooded
With children.

Issa's haiku captures the joyful aftermath of winter as children play in the melting snow, evoking a sense of renewal and the cyclical nature of seasons. His work often reflects on the human condition with a tender and empathetic touch.

These masters of haiku have inspired countless poets worldwide, including myself. Their ability to distill complex emotions and vivid imagery into such brief forms is a testament to the power of simplicity. In "Rustling Leaves," I strive to honor their legacy by bringing the essence of haiku into the modern world, exploring themes that are timeless and universal.

In the gentle whisper of the wind through the trees, the world speaks in a language of subtlety and grace. "Rustling Leaves," a collection of Haiku verses as rendered unto English, is an ode to the quiet moments that often pass unnoticed yet carry the profound essence of our shared human experience.

Haiku, a traditional form of Japanese poetry, captures fleeting instants in nature with simplicity and depth. In just seventeen syllables, a haiku distills the essence of a scene, a feeling, or a thought, creating a vivid snapshot that lingers in the reader's mind. This collection embraces that tradition while allowing the nuances of the English language to breathe new life into it.

Each haiku in this book is a reflection of my journey through the seasons of life, an exploration of the beauty found in both the mundane and the extraordinary. The title, "Rustling Leaves," symbolizes the delicate yet powerful presence of nature's whispers, those moments that gently remind us of the interconnectedness of all things.

As you turn these pages, I invite you to pause and listen to the rustling leaves around you. Let the haiku guide you to a place of the subtle music of life comes forward. May these poems inspire you to find the extraordinary in the ordinary, and to appreciate the quiet beauty that exists in every moment?

As you read through this collection, I hope you will feel a connection to these great poets of the past and find your own moments of reflection and peace. May the spirit of Basho, Buson, and Issa whisper to you through the rustling leaves of these pages, and may their timeless wisdom inspire you as it has inspired me.

Thank you for embarking on this journey with me. May "Rustling Leaves" bring you peace, joy, and a deeper connection to the natural world and to your own inner landscape?

I deeply thank my friend, Mr. Amaran, a well-known poet who also laid his hand at translation in a few verses.

I would like to express my sincere thanks to P. Pillay Vyapoory GOSK, former Vice President of the Republic of Mauritius, for his great felicitation text for this book.

24-08-2024

With gratitude

Aathiran

aathiran108@gmail.com

At midnight–
A frog ashore...
Recognizing double moon!

Arise sun may, leisurely–
Dissolving now...
Night, and candle!

Reaching the mountain–
Nothing brought from below...
Except shadow

His mundane route–
Never did he hear
Today's harp – music!

Thou own a heart
Whilst the ocean, waves...
Rest, nowhere!

Now hurried spring–
Leaving summer behind...
Its haiku, I am writing!

The cascade roars–
Ah, whence to hear
The descending blossoms

A Hunchback, now–
As hidden in faded shadow
Mine youth

Summer moonlight
Translating,
Beauty of spring!

Visualizing fields nearby–
Away from distant hills,
The pretty cascade!

Gathering hues
For painting – realizing
Speedy vernal approach!

To copy the moon
Has to wait till night
Pond, fully water'd!

Unloading complicated thoughts–
Keeping erect seen
Excellent sun!

Whether summer or spring–
Only for thee awaits,
Bright moon!

Ever in drapes–
At times under water...
Mine nudity, hidden!

Awaiting spring?
Lo, hues pour'd
Everywhere!

Snow creeping o'er ridges–
Touches thee too... wherein
Water springs!

Mono – moon
With angles variegated...
Poetic everywhere!

Spread with enumerous stars...
Lo, fireflies all over
The dark jungle!

Despite hunger and snow–
Visit vernal world once...
At least by imagination!

However distant be–
No end to sky
And time dissolved fully

Viewing sky–
Minute stars from hence...
Ah, from thence?

Having advanced so far
In forest... no dreading of flood!
Aware of an ant on yellow leaf?

Silent fall!
For the sake of a flower
How scream rusting leaves!

No snatching away–
Let the cannonball tree
With its flower spread divinity!

With cold, bones chill'd–
However in void mine house
Myself, fulfill'd!

Snow creeping o'er dawn–
Withdrawing self
How divine the beauty!

In hauling a single fish
How joyous the mono – legged crane ...
Melancholic, indeed!

A glorious sight–
Double-petalled, it blossomed...
The butterfly!

Only one pond–
Reflecting both the sun
And moon smilingly!

So happy its fight–
The rainy termite... despite
Fallen life within a day!

Both slept, thou
And the cat... anyone
Witnessed slumber of aquarium – fish?

Nature alive
Howsoever even be cold... and
Motionless me!

Single moon
For multi-stars? or
Only moon for stars all

Light if beautiful
Litting night...
Darkness, more fine!

Hovel, being torn
Enters moonlight... itself
Hidden somewhere!

Ah, passerby–
What's there to learn
From thee expert unfair truth!

Ah, dragonflies!
Where's thine destination
Beyond spring?

Thine journey!
Thou are to cross tree...
That enjoys thee!

Not at all a voice
In void... as wind
Passes thro' bamboo!

Its beyond thine doors–
That the world
Outside both extend!

Longing for goats, penned–
Untie them!
Thorny hill in fret!

The singe boat–
For whom awaits
Swaying in wind – Bound!

Ah flutter this little
Flower – So surprised,
The hued flowers at butterfly!

See sans hues–
Only during day time
It's full – Blown Blue!

Tank with water,
Fully stock'd... whither
The flock of birds in migration

Spent fields!
Ah, the farmer's haul of
Their labour!

Shehnai – music
Though not meant for me...
Postpones mine sleeping hours!

Come summer may
No botheration...
Spring's spirited for thee!

With spittle builds
Its nest... and the wasp – definitely
Aware of our silk – manufacture!

She whilst enjoying
From bedroom... amused at
Moon- viewing from courtyard!

Why explain nature
Of water borne fish – he,
Accustom'd to desert!

Thou dare not touch
The moon...lo, tank fisher,
Distorting the same!

Rain cleared–
In leaves rustling,
Its rain, again!

What all it blossom'd
Enjoyment, complete
Of spring season!

Hot summer – whilst
I search o'er empty
Rice pot... sky wails in void!

Till it reaches nostrils–
Fragrance of flowers,
Transmitted by wind – not known!

Here's dark jungle
Whilst heavy snow, elstwhere...
Myself, all alone!

Drought – Prone summer...
As earth wears flower – drape... he,
Engaged in drawing!

The sun–
Drawing a portrait
Of mine shadow!

Day lingers–
As moon appears... even's
Beauty beyond description!

Carrying umbrella against rain–
Playing in rainy – street
Beauties, differentiated!

Rustling whilst
Walking... what'd be
The leaves' talk?

Only a few flowers
Predict changes...
Ah, seasons against times!

Whence the light,
If guessed proper...
Whither lightning

Mine mind, a steed
Knows not how
To enjoy – the spring moon!

Traversing light–
Whither and whence
The fireflies

Dashing against showers–
Flowering of bubbles
Against – blossoming buds!

Leaving darkness
Behind... whither
Hurries – the sun!

Pretty evening–
As she lingers at
Other shore, summer's double moon!

Moonlit night–
Heavy with snow,
Myself, awaken'd!

Coffee – cup...
In evaporation chillness
Solaced... Snowy night!

Pure desert–
How sprouts a seed,
Branching out in confidence!

Against joyous boomering
Of beetles... its time
I seek mine harp!

Ah, I'm in search
Haiku that
Vanish'd like lightning!

Moon – Full of Meaning
Or nil – availing
Views, variegated

Light – in the process
Of driving away darkness – no
Other go, I'll await!

A boat – Trip!
Howsoever left ashore–
Mind, still swimming!

Listening to the voice
Of cascade... aware
Of rhythmic – muse?

Night sans light–
Clearly visualized
Via mind's eye!

Just to welcome
Vernal arrival... withering of
A few flowers and leaves!

In autumn and
In chillness... whither
Thine presence, vernal breeze

As nostrils cherish
Vernal fragrance... Its
Raining somewhere!

Forest portrayed in
Beauty via painted
Feathers of the butterfly!

If thou talk – they
Too converse accordingly...
An assumption, eeh!

Underfully – blown
Thee... summer's sunsine
Fond of blossom's shadow!

Whether noon or
Westward as sun moves...
Blossoms, awake in shade!

This note for those,
Following me... and those
Dreaded not of dreary nights!

Mine contemplation over
Thoughts of good old people...
Moon, alive!

As it drizzles
Beyond late night... ah,
None to enjoy!

Chillness, unbearable–
What all I need now... come,
Fill the tea-cup!

In touching and
In realizing touch...
Emotions, ennmerous!

As beetles drowse in blossoms–
So also men in wine shop...
Spring, ahead!

Wither'd leaves o'er
Entire courtyard... oh yes!
Autumn, season'd!

Thou shalt pronounce
A secret... even as
I expose one... beautiflying entire night!

Touch me soft with
Peacock's feathers... or else
Send me – the breeze!

As fluctuates soil–
So sprouts,
The seed!

Multi-hued flower – plants...
Attempting to capture colours
On its feathers – the butterfly!

Grains, if dampen'd!
So saddened... wails
The sky overhead!

Sunbird since
Biulds nest... windows
Not to open nowadays!

For notes

For notes

About the Author

Name of Author	: **Dr. R. Arulraj**
Nickname	: **Aathiran**
Education	: **M.Sc., M.Phil., Ph.D. (Chemistry), M.A. (Tamil)**
Mother's Name	: **R. Rani**
Father's Name	: **S. Ramalingam**
Work	: He has held positions such as manager in multinational pharmaceutical companies and research fellow at the National University of Singapore.

Website: https://sites.google.com/view/aathirankavithaigal/home

Books Published

2024

- Paruvam Neendathoru Muththam
  (Haiku Poetry collections in Tamil)
- Minnal Pookkum Pozhuthugal
  (A collection of poems in Tamil)

2023

- 3033 (Futuristic World in an unpredictable universe)
  (A collection of Short Stories in English)

Awards Received

2024

- June 9th – "Haiku Peroli Award", Tamil Haiku 3rd conference 2024, World Tamil Sangam, Madurai.
- April 28th – "Kavi Thendral Award", Tamizharuvi Vanoli Yermeni and Sanga Tamizh Ilakkiya Poonga, Pavendar Bharathidasan Vizha, Puduvai Tamizh Sangam, Puducherry
- March 10th – Senthamizh Semmal Award", Kamban Kazhagam, France & Sanga Tamizh Ilakkiya Poonga, Chennai.
- February 21st – "Tamil Thesiya Pattraalar Award", Veerathamirasi Velunachyar Literary Society Movement, Puducherry.
- February 4th – "Semmozhich Selvam Virudhu", World Mother Language Day Series Event, Sanga Tamil Ilakkiya Poongaa, Chennai.

- February 1st – "Assist World Achievement Certificate of Participation", 75 Hours Series Assist World Achievement, Puduvai Arasu Kalaimamani Awardee Society, Puducherry.
- January 16th - Valluvar Thondar Apprecition Certificate, Tirukkural Festival - Valluvar Salutation Program, Sanga Tamil Ilakkiya Poongaa, Chennai

2023

- September 21st to 26th – "Bainthamizh Therppagan Award" Second World Poets Conference, Ministry of Culture and Fine Arts, Department of Culture and Fine Arts, and Angkor Tamil Sangam, Siam Reap, Cambodia.
- December 26th – "Kalai Rathna Award - 2023 [Iyal]", Puduvai Arasu Kalaimamani Awardee Society, Puducherry.

2022

- 2022 - "Ilam Kavignar Thanga Muththirai Award and Gold Medal", Kavimalai, Singapore.

Contribution in other Books

- 2024 – Ondodi Kanne, Sanga Pookkal - 4, World Record Tamil Poetry Collection, Sanga Thamizh Ilakkiya Poongaa, Coimbatore.
- 2021 – Maouna Vithaigal (Tamil Poetry Collection), Kavimaalai Singapore.

- 2019 – Antha Oru Sol (Tamil Poetry Collection), Kavimaalai Singapore.
- 2017 – September 9, Singapor Kathambam (Short Stories Collection in Tamil), Uyirmei Pathippagam, National Library, Singapore.
- 2017 – Azhagu Magudam (Poetry Collection), Kavimaalai Singapore.

Journal Paper Publications (Tamil & General)

- Dr. Arulraj Ramalingam, Review on Ancient Tamil Architecture: A Immortal Heritage of Creativity and Artistic Perfection, Shanlax International Journal of Arts, Science and Humanities, 11(4), Apr 2024, doi: https://doi.org/10.34293/sijash.v11i4.7348.

Journal Paper Publications (Science)

- He has more than 30 scientific papers that have been published in various international scientific journals.
- Google Scholar: https://scholar.google.com/citations?user=KRTSrbIAAAAJ&hl=en